NERD LOVE

The Cookbook

ISBN: 978-1-387-26078-2

Thank you

This book is for my dad. He may have not completely understood this nerd thing. He always supported me and loved me. This was a labor of love.wish you could have seen it.

Mom, thanks for putting up with all my strange ideas and help flesh out this book.

For the rest of my family for just going with the nerd love. Jamie,Jackie,Jared and Avery, I love you guys

For everyone who has listened to me talk about my love for food, nerds and life. Thanks

I am so blessed to have the knowledge and experiences to write this great cookbook. Also to be able to share this. So I thank those who are reading this.

The list of awesome. Nathan s, josh and robin, Vinnie, Jake, terry and Gwen,krista,will,c,chia,Greg and all the guys at the shop. All my fellow nerd and my lord and savior Jesus Christ

I am a nerd. What is a nerd? It is someone who is passionate about a certain part of pop culture. Be that comic book, tv, movie or even a certain character. The even will go as far as desiring to be the character. To celebrate that fandom with friends and family. To even go as far as have foods from that fandom.

I also love food. I love to eat it, cook it, talk about it and experience it in any way possible. As someone who loves food it comes natural for it to crossover to my fandoms. If that is having a theme dinner when playing a tabletop role playing game. Or some fun and creative snacks for a watch party for your favorite tv show. A lot of times it just giving easy -remade snacks a makeover or some internet recipe that is complicated or non sensical. So her I try to give good recipes that are not only easy to do but taste good. So first why is this call the nerd love cook book.

Nerd love is a nonprofit that's goal is to advocating positivity, confidence in self and others and excitement in nerd culture with all the things nerds love. To build a positive ,open and all inclusive community. Using the love of Comic books, television, movies, cosplay, gaming, and any fandom to promoting positive body image, community activities, anti-bulling , local get-togethers, supporting comic cons and making sure all people are able to enjoy their fandoms. We do this through supporting cosplayer and there rights, advocating comic convention manners and sharing positive new about nerd culture. The desire is to form a positive and growing community for anyone who consider them self nerdy.

I believe Food brings us together. It is the center of any party,celebration or get together. When our favorite fandom has something to celebrate. We want to share it. What's better than to have food that goes with it. This book gives recipes to help you enjoy your fandoms with your friends. With each chapter I not only bring great recipes with fun twist but also tips on how to make the celebrations great. Also just the recipes the self are real good food. I believe that good food should be as fresh as possible. So I give as many from scratch recipe as possible. You can use short cuts if necessary no judging from me. I believe these are high quality recipes. I also think buying good ingredients makes for good food.

The recipes are inspired buy broad categories of fandoms across the nerd world. From silly to kind of gross. That's the fun part. Having as much fun as possible while still having good food. Each recipe has been tested and shared with my friends and family when we celebrate our fandoms. These recipes are also good food. I have used my skills and knowledge of the culinary world to have easy,good quality recipes you can make and enjoy.

Nerd food basics

Fantasy recipes

Halloween recipes

Steampunk recipes

Superhero recipes

Snack recipes

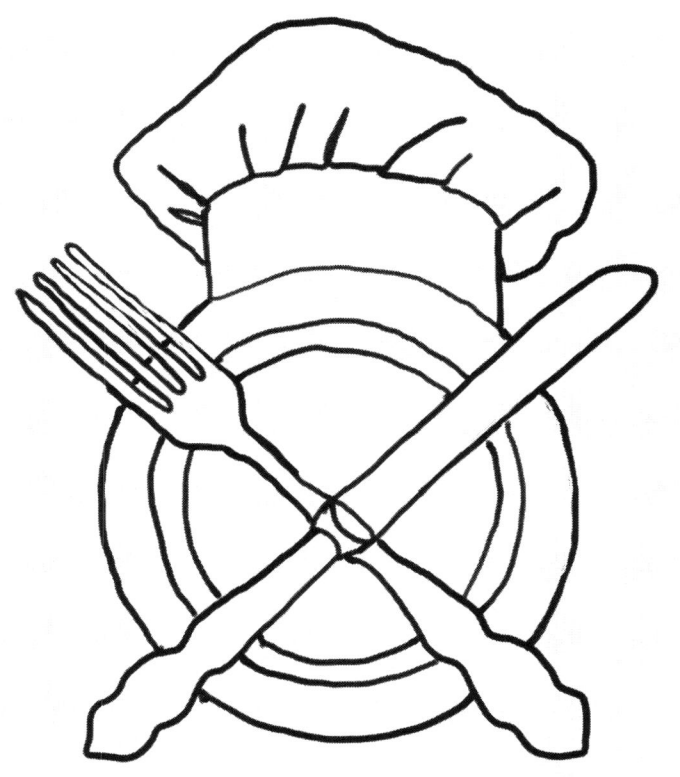

This book is for food nerds or for nerds who love food. The recipes in this book are to help you celebrate your fandom with pride. Also with a lot of fun. The first thing is what is a food nerd. It is a person with not only a passion for good food, but a passion to make good food and serve that food to your friends and family. To start that passion, here are a few basic recipes to help you become a food nerd. These are all recipes that you can by prepared but are so much more satisfying when you make it from scratch with your own hands. Some of these recipes are used in the book. Some are just great recipes to have access to.

*1.*We can all go buy instant pudding but from scratch pudding allows you to be in charge of taste. This is for vanilla but just by adding canned fruit, fresh fruit, chocolate or Carmel to make it awesome. Eat this by itself, use in a pie crust, or in another desert.

Pudding

2 cups Milk

1 cup White sugar

2 tablespoon Cornstarch

1 teaspoon Salt

2 table spoon Butter

3 tablespoons vanilla

Pudding

1.In sauce pan cook milk till bubbling at sides

2.combine sugar cornstarch and salt, take milk off heat

3.slowly add dry mix to milk.put back on heat

4.add butter and vanilla, do not boil

5.chill pudding till cold.

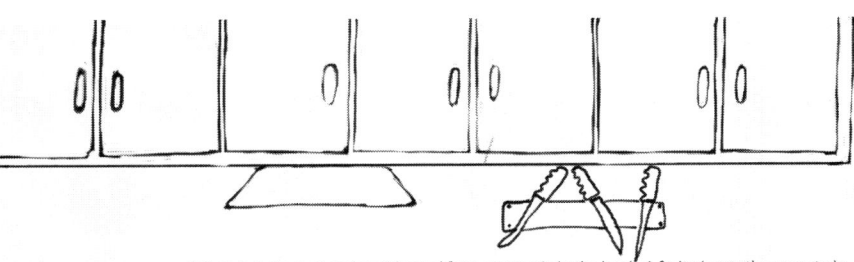

2. Here is a pie crust recipe. It is used for a savory pie in the book. A fruit pie or other sweet pie will be good for this recipe.

Crust

1 1/4 cups all-purpose flour

1/4 teaspoon salt

1/2 cup butter, chilled and diced

1/4 cup ice water

Add all ingredients to list

Directions

In a large bowl, combine flour and salt. Cut in butter until mixture resembles coarse crumbs. Stir in water, a tablespoon at a time, until mixture forms a ball. Wrap in plastic and refrigerate for 4 hours or overnight.

Roll dough out to fit a 9 inch pie plate. Place crust in pie plate. Press the dough evenly into the bottom and sides of the pie plate.

3. I believe that making your own pickles are so much better. Adding onions, button mushrooms or peppers to add flavor or color.

Pickle and onions
1 cup apple cider vinegar

- 1/8 cup salt
- 1 cup white sugar
- 1/4 teaspoon ground turmeric
- 1/2 teaspoon mustard seed
- 2 pounds cucumbersCucumber
- 2 sweet onions

Pickle

1. In a small saucepan at medium-high heat, combine cider vinegar, salt, sugar, tumeric and mustard seed. Bring to a boil and let cook for 5 more minutes.
2. Meanwhile, slice cucumbers and onion. Loosely pack the vegetables in a 1-quart canning jar or other similarly sized container. Pour hot liquid over the vegetables in the container. Refrigerate for 24 hours and enjoy! Keep refrigerated.

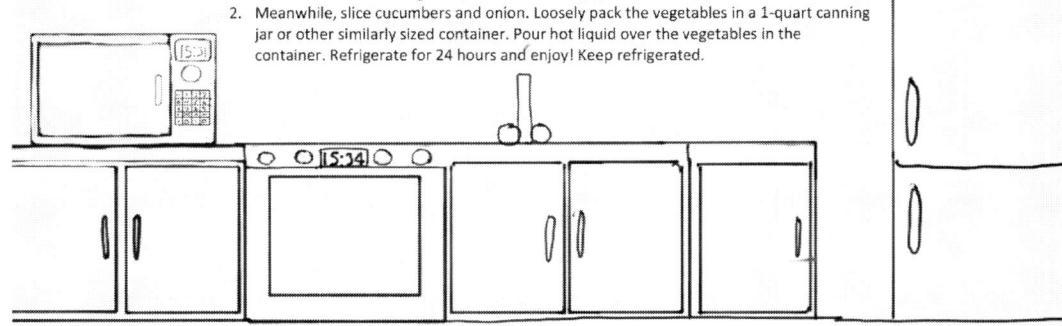

4. This is a simple and easy pizza crust for any pizza.

3 cups all-purpose flour or Better

1. tablespoon sugar

1 teaspoon salt

1 package regular or quick active dry yeast
(2 1/4 teaspoons)

1 tablespoons olive or vegetable oil
1 cup very warm water (120° to 130°
Toppings

pizza dough
1.Mix 1 cup of the flour, the sugar, salt and yeast in large bowl. Add 3 tablespoons oil and the
warm water. Beat with electric mixer on medium speed 3 minutes, scraping bowl frequently.
Stir in enough remaining flour until dough is soft and leaves sides of bowl. Place dough on
lightly floured surface. Knead 5 to 8 minutes or until dough is smooth and springy. Cover loosely
with plastic wrap and let rest 30 minutes.
2.cut into 1 inch balls
3.Roll each ball thin and put stuffing in center and fold

4.cook until crispy brown

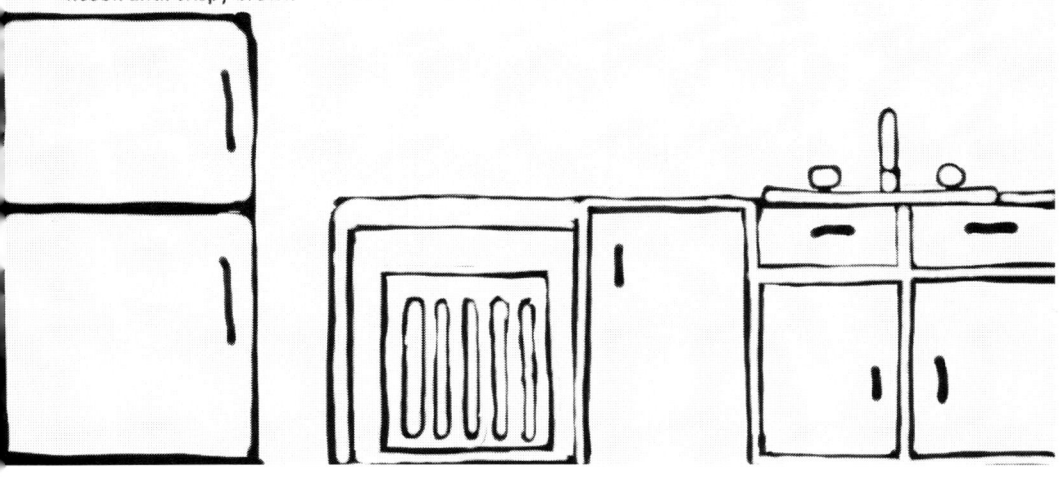

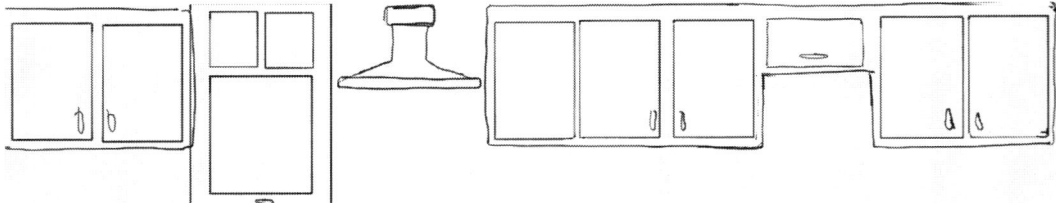

5. All real foodies make their own pizza sauce. This is a great sauce for pizza or pasta.

Pizza sauce

- 1 to 2 tablespoons olive oil
- 3 cloves garlic, minced
- 1 medium onion, chopped finely
- 1/2 cup chicken broth
- Three 15-ounce cans crushed tomatoes
- Salt and pepper
- Pinch sugar
- 1 teaspoon dried oregano
- 8 to 10 fresh basil leaves, chopped

Sauce

Add a tablespoon or so of olive oil into a hot pan over medium-high heat. Throw in the garlic and chopped onions and give them a stir. Cook until the onions are soft, 4 to 5 minutes. Add the chicken broth, whisking to deglaze the bottom of the pan. Cook until the liquid reduces by half. Add the crushed tomatoes and stir to combine. Add salt and pepper to taste and a pinch of sugar. Add the dried oregano and basil. Reduce the heat to low and simmer for 30 minutes.

6. I believe a good sausage can make or break a dish. This recipe allows you to be picky with what you put into to this assuage.
Sausage
Sausage

- 2 pounds pork butt (2 1/2 pounds with bone), diced into 1/4-inch pieces
- 2 teaspoons kosher salt
- 1 1/2 teaspoons freshly ground black pepper
- 2 teaspoons finely chopped fresh sage leaves
- 2 teaspoons finely chopped fresh thyme leaves
- 1/2 teaspoon finely chopped fresh rosemary leaves
- 1 tablespoon light brown sugar
- 1/2 teaspoon fresh grated nutmeg
- 1/2 teaspoon cayenne pepper
- 1/2 teaspoon red pepper flakes
- 1/4 teaspoon dried marjoram
- 1 pinch ground cloves

Mix all dried ingredients in bowl.
Add pork into dried ingredients. Chill for one hour
Cook until light brown
Drain and cool

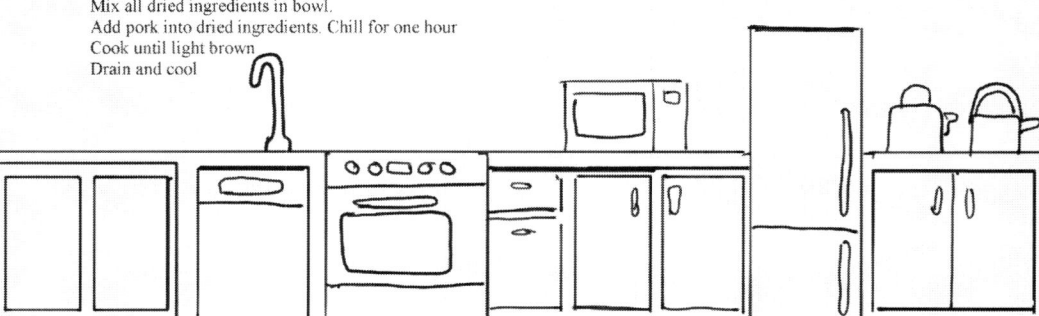

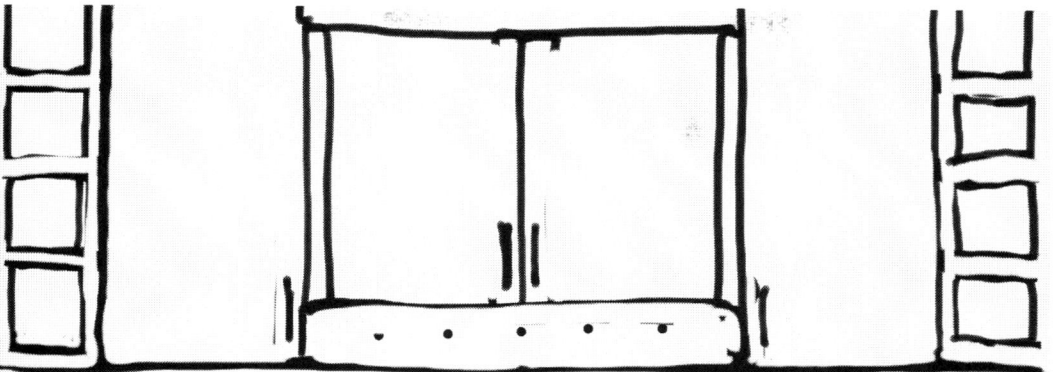

6. This jam is actually pretty good but you can remove the tomatoes or replace them and make any type of jam.

Strawberry tomato jam

- 4 cups diced beefsteak tomatoes (2 to 3 large tomatoes)
- 1 1/2 cups chopped strawberries
- 1 cup sugar
- 1/8 teaspoon ground cinnamon
- 1/8 teaspoon kosher salt
- 1 teaspoon fresh lemon juice

Place the diced tomatoes in a medium saucepan over medium-high heat and bring to a boil. Reduce the heat to a simmer and add the strawberries, sugar, cinnamon, salt and lemon juice. Stir to combine. Bring to a simmer and cook over medium-low heat, stirring occasionally, until the mixture has thickened to the consistency of a loose jam, 40 to 45 minutes. Set aside to cool completely.

FANTASY RECIPES

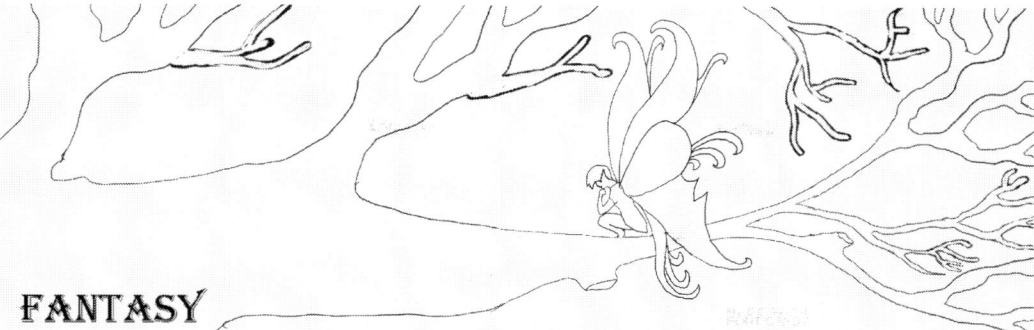

FANTASY

To throw a great fantasy party you need to not only have great for but the dishes and Devore need to be as awesome as the food. These recipes will give you a great menu for your fantasy party. If you desire a great meal to go along your fantasy rpg. Your going to have a awesome watch party for your favorite fantasy movie or tv show. The dragon tail and the other recipes are great for any occasion but especially if you want to be the king or queen of your own kingdom.

Here are some great tips to accompany this awesome fantasy foods.

1. If you can do an outdoor party use a tent. Decorate tent with plastic weapons and plastic armor.. Also use dark color fabric to hang on side of tent and put on table. Also can make small flags and divide your guest into family's.

2. indoor you can use a dark color sheet and attach over table your using for food like a tent. You can use a medieval looking flag as a table cloth. If not sitting guest at a single table. You can cover your furniture with clothes and dark color blankets on your floor for a royal sitting area.

3. You can use fake black birds on the table or chairs for a dark magic feel. Also find small fish bowl and put clear rope lights on bottom and turn bowl upside down on them to use as a crystal ball center piece

4. Create a draw bridge at the entrance to your party ,your front door or yard gate using plywood. Attach chains to the plywood and door frame area, in an open draw bridge fashion.

5. Line the walkway or hallway with torches and place a few throughout the party rooms.

6. For a festive entrance, line your walkway with colorful flags. You can create them from construction paper, card stock, or felt. Attach them to skinny wood dowels and push the dowels into the ground.

7. Make a royal throne for your party by attaching a tall piece of plywood to a chair. Cover with purple velvet or satin fabric. Decorate chair with jewels, sequins, glitter, etc. then have fun party games to see who gets to be king or queen of party.

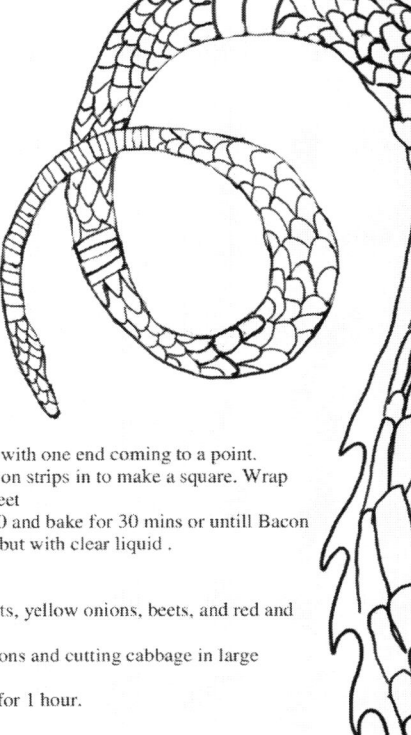

Dragon tale

Ingredients

1 5 pound beef or pork tenderloin
1 pound sweet ground pork sausage
1 pound thin cut apple wood bacon
2 oz honey mustard
2 oz horseradish sauce

Directions'
1.brown tenderloin on all sides in iron skillet
2.combine mustard and horseradish and cover tenderloin
3.wrap tenderloin with sausage. Make sure its a thin layer with one end coming to a point.
4.lay 4 bacon pieces side by side. Then weave another bacon strips in to make a square. Wrap around tenderloin. Wrap in foil Lay on rack on baking sheet
5.bake at 350 for 1 hour. In wrap foil. Increase heat to 400 and bake for 30 mins or untill Bacon is be crisp. The tenderloin should have a slight pink color but with clear liquid .

Serve with roasted root vegetables.
1. Use vegetables like white, orange and purple carrots, yellow onions, beets, and red and green cabbage.
2. Clean and prepare buy pealing carrots. pealing onions and cutting cabbage in large chunks.
3. Cover in olive oil then   Roast on flat pain on 375 for 1 hour.

Decorating tips
1.Use Easter eggs to decorate table. The larger the better
2spray paint your eggs with some white spray paint/primer that is meant to stick to plastic. Easy, dries quick.
3.paint your newly primed eggs any color you want a good place to start is in various shades of green, purple, gold. Let the acrylic paint dry for a little while
4. The dragon scale pattern is just drawn on with black Sharpie. Preferably nice, new crisp black Sharpies – and be prepared to go through at least a couple of them. draw the pattern on your eggs lightly in pencil, THEN go over it in Sharpie. If you want a thicker line like some of ours, just go over it again

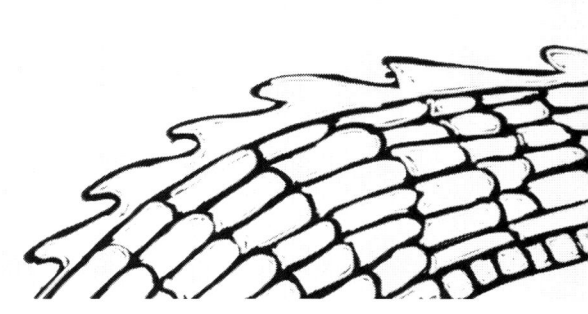

Dragon eggs

Ingredients
6 eggs
1 large pot of water
1 cup Worcestershire sauce
2 chi tea bags

Filling
2 tablespoons mustard
2 tablespoon horseradish
3 drops hot sauce

Directions

1. boil eggs for 5 mins
2. crack shell but do not remove
3. Refill pot with 1cup water, Worcestershire and tea bags. Bring to boil
4. Put eggs back in water for another 5 min so liquid can absorb in to egg
5. Remove eggs from water and pill, eggs should have dark lines
6. Split egg long ways
7. remove yoke
8. Mix yoke, mustard, horseradish and hot sauce until creamy
9. Pipe filling into one side of egg and put two sides back together

Serve on a bed of red cabbage leaves spread on a platter.

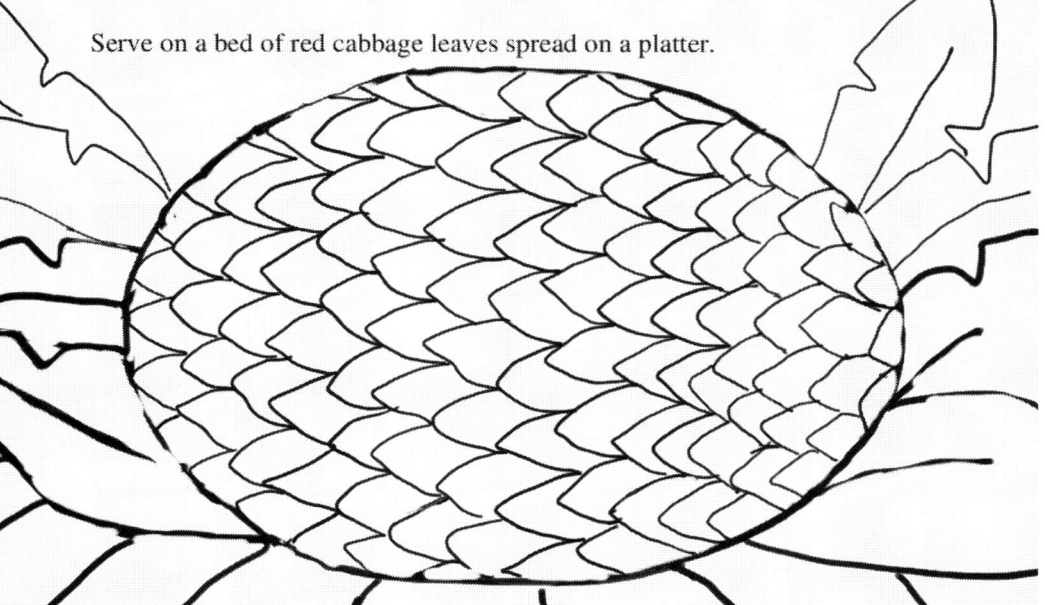

Day mead

Ingredients

21 ounces apple juice
42 ounces honey
63 ounces water
2 tablespoons fresh ginger
2 tablespoons cinnamon
2 table spoons orange slices
2 table spoons nutmeg

Directions
1.Putt all ingredients in non metal container and bring to boil
2.simmer for 10 mins
3.drain and refrigerate until cool

Serve as a drink in masion jars

 use as a marinade a whole chicken in day mead for 3 hours the roast for one hour in 350 oven

Also can add 2 cups to a pot and reduce with a cup of sugar till half gone. Cool and use as a
syrup for baked apples or pears. Bake fruit cored with butter in core and outside for 1 hour on
350

Potatoes roasted in dragons blood

Ingredients
10 to 12 small red roasting potatoes
2 cloves minced garlics
3 tablespoons finely chopped ginger
2 tablespoons black pepper
3 tablespoons hot sauce
3 cups strong red wine
Butter

Directions
1.slice potatoes thin and add in boiling water. Boil for three mins. Remove potatoes in to baking pan.pre heat oven to 350
2.in sauce pan, on medium heat, add 1 table butter garlic and ginger. cook till light drown.
3. then add red wine and black pepper until boil.
4.Add hot sauce on low heat.Reduce for 5min then Pour over potatoes . 4.Roast for 45 min on 375

Serve with dragon tail or as a side dish to a roasted chicken.

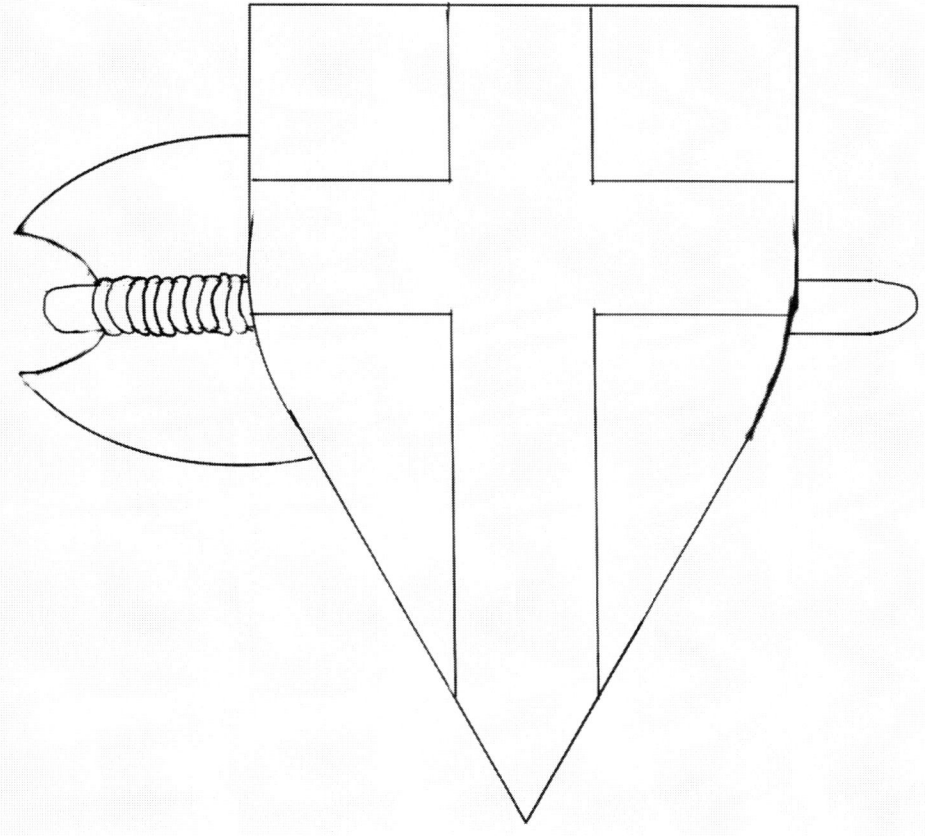

Blood snow

Ingediants

For Toping
1 cup whipped topping
Vanilla pudding mixture

For Pudding
2 cups Milk
1 cup White sugar
2 tablespoon Cornstarch
1 teaspoon Salt
2 table spoon Butter
3 tablespoons vannila

For Berry mixture
1 pound strawberries
1/2 cup white sugar
1 cup balsamic vinegar

Direction
Topping
Combine pudding mix and whip topping. Refigerate

Pudding
1.In sauce pan cook milk till bubbling at sides
2.combine sugar cornstarch and salt, take milk off heat
3.slowly add dry mix to milk.put back on heat
4.add butter and vanilla, do not boil
5.chill pudding till cold.

Berry mixture
1.chop berry in a small dice
2.add sugar and vinaigrette in sauce pan. Heat till sugar is melted. Add strawberrys
3.cook for 5 min
4.cool mixture

In large glass bowl add berry mixture as first layer, then pudding, then topping

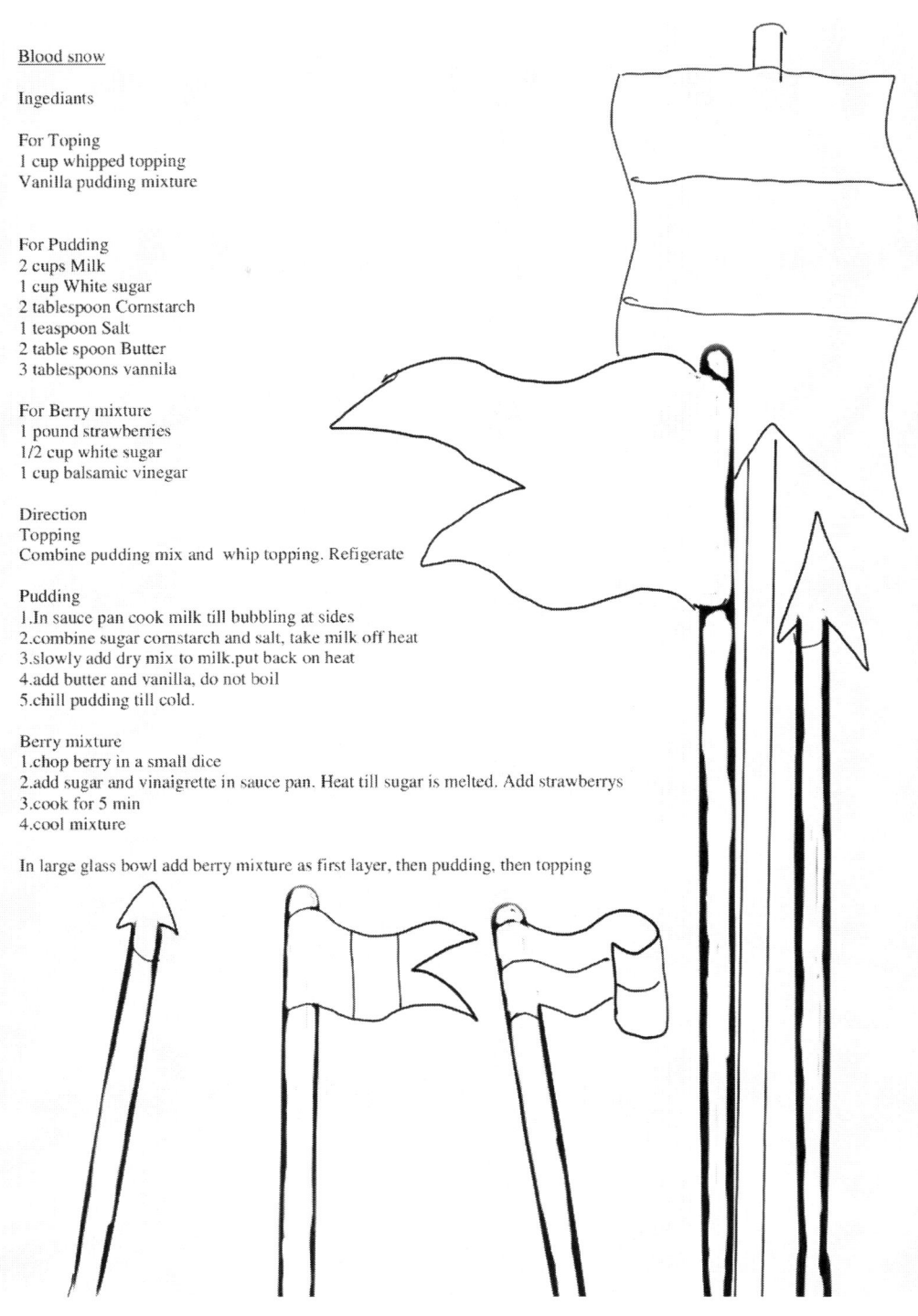

HALLOWEEN RECIPES

Halloween or All Hallows' eve is possible the biggest celebration for nerd there is. It's a time when everyone is dressing up and thinking about ghost and goblins. So if your planning a huge party, a small get together or just watching a bunch of horror films. Here is a group of recipes that will make your next Halloween party the creepiest there is. Below are some great party tips and treats to make it the spookiest time of the year.

This food looks great with a mad sciences theme on you tables. You can go as far as finding cheap beakers to drink from. Also if you want to you can use peter dishes to eat on. Clean one of course. Fill the room with white sheets on your tables and lab coats for your guest to wear.

i think the grosser the better with this meal. This can easily be toned down on the gross factor. Easy ways are to not add a lot of sause to the meatloaf or forgo the sause completely. To up the gross factor with the meatloaf. Add a small layer of meat to the mold. Then in the fingers and hand line with the shallots to look like bones the finish filling and cook like normal.

Some cool table decorations for the table can be done with ease. Use fave vampire teeth to hold nice napkins or silver wear bundles.Use spider rings in ice cubes for drinks. Cut off rings then freeze in punch recipe in ice tray. Also you Can put long tapered candles in clear coke or wine bottles around table cloth.

If adding dips to your party for appetizers. Try use plastic skulls as dish. Cut top. Line with plastic baggy for easy cleanup and fill with dip. If you can find plastic skeleton hands . Clean them well first and attach to a plastic bowl. Either a cheap one and glue them on or if using a nicer plater use tape ten fill with chips.

The meat hand is a great center piece of any Halloween party. This is for a more seat down dinner party also great for a movie party. If the hand creeps you out. You can do this in a loaf pan and pour half of sauces on top before baking. Then when done pour over meatloaf for a bloody meatloaf.

Meat hand

1 pound ground hand burger meat
1 pound ground chicken
1 cup pinko bread crumbs
1 bunch parsley
1 cup fresh basil
1 cup hot mustard
2 eggs

Sauce for top
1 can tomato paste
1 cup brown sugar
3 tablespoons sisters hire sauce
1/2 cup hot mustard
1/2 cup apple cider vinegar
2 tablespoon hot sauce

To make hand mold
Trace hand with permanent marker on parchment paper.
Cut out hand print. Wrap foil around each hand to make sides of finger and hand. Do three to for layers until stiff.

Instructions
Spray mold with cooking oil.
Place all ingredients in bowl and mix well.place in mold. Place mold on cookie sheet. Bake for 45 min on 350 degrees. Take out of oven and invert meatloaf and then peal off foil. Put two slices of American cheese on top , insert shallot half way into flat end of hand and cook for another 10 minutes.

Cool on wire rack
To make Sauce
Combine all ingredients and mix until no lumps.
Chill until read to serve

Use for dipping meat loaf or pour over if not using mashed potatoes
This recipe is great on its on. Instead of the American cheese you can use a better melting chees like a sharp cheddar or a provolone. Using the American cheese is for the bubbling effect that makes it look like burnt cheese.

Blood punch

If your not wanting to use soda of any kind you can just use the punch. Any punch will do but the recipe for the handmade is fantastic. To make it more adult use a hard cola and some maraschino cherry syrup. The cherries floating it it look great too. you can play with the measurements. Just don't freeze the soda parts.

Ingredients
1 gallonFruits punch
1 cup Granada
1 cup cherry doctor pepper
1 cup Ginger ale
1 jar maraschino cherries

Fruit punch recipe
2 cups Cranberry juice
2 cups Orange juice
1 Lemonade froze concentrate
2 cupsPineapple juice
Juice from maraschino cherries
Apple juice
Non powdered latex glove

Directions
Fill latex gloves with punch, freeze for six hours

Combine ingredients and chill

Remove glove from freezer. Add glove to punch bowl. Fill with the rest of mix in the bowl including the rest of the punch

This is a simple dessert. You can add gummy worms for a bit of fun. Another way to serve is in clear plastic cups. With masking tape on side.write where the sample came from.

<u>Graveyard dirt samples</u>
Homemade marsh mellow cream
2 egg whites at room temperature
1/2 cup corn syrup
1/2 cup powder sugar
3 tablespoon vanilla
1 tablespoon salt
Homemade chocolate pudding
1 cup sugar
1 1/2 cup coco powder
3 cups milk
3 tablespoon vanilla
5 tablespoon cornstarch

Chocolate gram cracker crumb
Coco powder
Gram cracker

Direction
Marshmallow cream
1.in bowl stir egg whites and corn syrup till soft peaks. Add vanilla and stir
2.slowly add powder sugar until combined. Refrigerate
Pudding
3.in sauce pan combined sugar, coco and cornstarch.
4.slowly add milk.
5.remove from heat add butter and vanilla
6.put in large serving bowl and refrigerate for 3 hours.
7.add marshmallows cream on top of chocolate
8.in plastic bag, add coco and gram crackers. Seal bag and crush.
Add to top of marshmallows
 Premade marshmallow cream will work. It is a little sweeter than the Homemade but will cut off about 20 minutes of prep time.

These mashed potatoes not only look great with the meatloaf but taste great also. Not patting the spinach dry will give a good color. If you want them greener use a drop of green food coloring

Moldy mashed potatoes
Ingredients
4 table spoons butter
1 cup cream
4 russet potatoes
1 package of chopped spinach

Instructions
1.boil 1 inch cube potatoes with peel in 2 quarts water
2.defrost package spinach. Do not pat dry.
3.drain potatoes. Add butter and cream and mash with fork. Mash till similar smooth.
4.add spinach and stir till mixed well. Add spinach water for more moister.

instead of spinach you can use collard green, char or herds like parsley and green onions for the color

Finger food

This is a cool and creepy twist on the classic party food, pigs in a blanket. The onion is a great little detail to make it extra creepy. Putting this on a bed of lettuce on a platter with the dipping sauce.

Crescent roll
Little sausage
Onion

For dip
Horseradish sauce
Tomato paste
Black pepper
Hot sauce

Homemade horseradish sauce

- 2 tablespoons prepared horseradish
- 1 tablespoon cider vinegar
- 1 teaspoon dry mustard
- 3 tablespoons reduced-fat mayonnaise
- 1/8 teaspoon ground red pepper
- 1/2 cup nonfat sour creaM

Directions

In a small bowl whisk together horseradish, vinegar, mustard, mayonnaise, ground red pepper and sour cream.

Directions
Take small onion and cut in small triangle.n cut out s thin section to look like a nail bed. Then, make a few cuts with a knife to represent the knuckles Place a piece of onion on tip of rolled sausage. Wrap sausage in strip pieces of crescent roll make it look like gross wrapping a finger leave in some areas exposed and leaving one end exposed.

Sauce
Combined horseradish sauce with tomato paste and hot sauce and serve cold

STEAMPUNK RECIPES

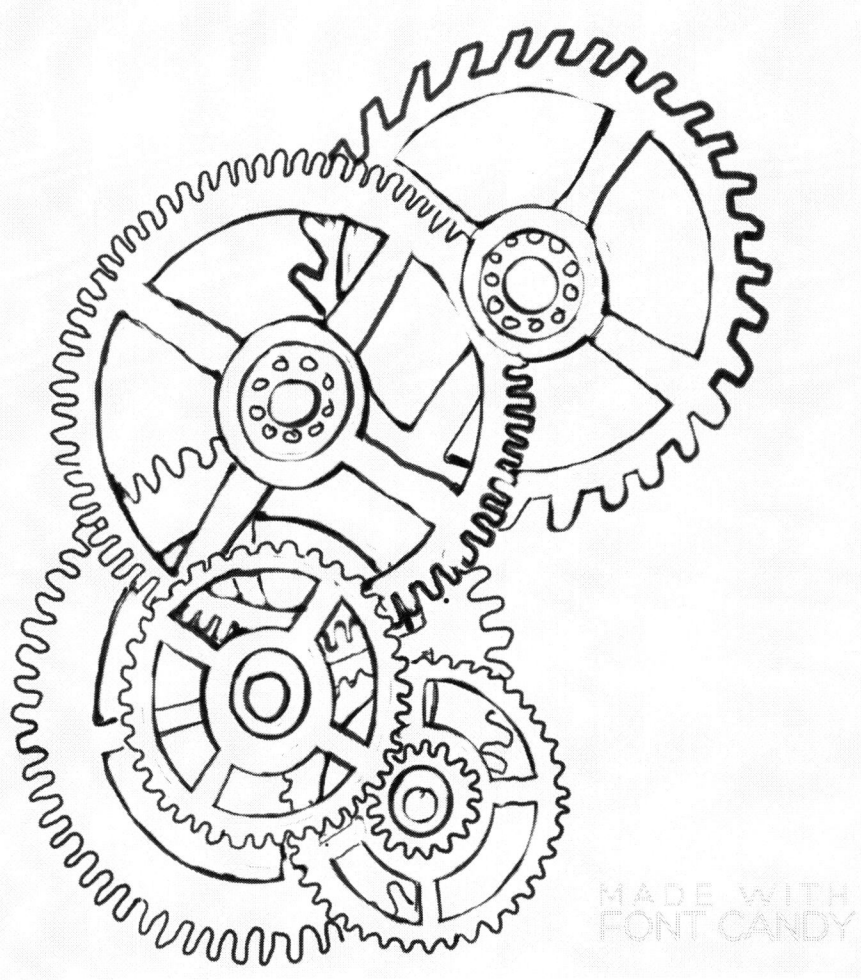

Steampunk is all the fun of brass, early electrify and other cool gadgets and gizmos with the fashion Sense of 109s England. Top hats, corsets and fancy suits and dresses. The food for this steampunk chapter is inspired by the food of the time period with a modern flair. This should be a elegant affair. Gentlemen in suits and ladies in large hoop dresses.

For decorating your house or party spot, use a mixture of antiques and found items with gears or exposed parts. Use Edison bulbs to help the look.

Watches, clocks, mechanical cogs, hot air balloons, motorcars, steam trains, and aviation are the main themes which influence steampunk. Pair these items with Victorian fabrics for your table, jacquard, light floral, lace etc. with heavy darker gothic inspired colors such as deep browns, reds and black.

Here is a list of Victorian games you can play.

Game 1. How? What? Where? When?

1. One player needs to think of the name of an object. Tip: Make it more difficult by thinking of a word with multiple meanings, like male (masculine), mail (letters) and mail (armor).

2. The other players try to discover what it is by asking (only once) the following four questions:

How do you like it?

Why do you like it?

When do you like it?

Where do you like it?

3. Player 1 must answer the questions truthfully. Alternate between the meanings as appropriate for each question.

4. The person who guesses correctly wins, and then takes the role of Player 1.

Game 2. Lookabout

The host shows everyone a little knick-knack in the room. All the guests are to leave while the host hides it. When they return, everyone is to look for the item until they spot it. They are then to sit down. The last one to find it loses (or has to be "it"). It makes it a bit more difficult if guests continue to mill for a few seconds before they sit down.

This is a great punch for a party where there are those who do not like alcoholic drinks. You can always have real drinks for the others. Serve in champagne glasses so no one feels left out in the party.

Champagne"punch

1 bottle of sparkling apple cider
1 cup of apple juice
2 teaspoons of Carmel syrup
Dry ice

1.First resolve the Carmel syrup in the apple juice by warming the juice in the microwave for 2 mins and stir till Carmel is gone.
2.cool apple juice before adding sparkling apple juice. Add then cool until you serve.
3. Carful;y add dry ice to durable punch bowl. The add cooled punch.

This is one of my favorite recipes in the book. It goes well with a steampunk or Victorian theme. This also goes well with any roasted proteins.

Cheesy corn

 2 10 -16 ounce) package frozen corn,
 3 tablespoons butter
 3 tablespoons flour
 2 cups cream
 2 Eggs
 1 cup crushed saltine crackers
 1/2 cup butter
 1/2 teaspoon paprika
 1/4 teaspoon ground black pepper
 1/2 teaspoon garlic powder
 1/2 teaspoon onion powder
 1 pound shredded cheddar cheese

Instructions
1.Melt butter in saucepan, stir in flour and blend well.
2.Add cream, about 1/2 cup at a time, and blend with whisk.
3.Cook over medium heat until thickened.
4.Stir in salt and pepper, garlic and onion powder
5.Add 1 package of thawed corn.
6.Put mixture in large casserole dish.
7.Add eggs, 1/4 cup of the melted butter and 1/2 of the cracker crumbs; 1/2 cup cheese,2nd package of corn into the dish with creamed corn mixture.
8.In a small bowl, mix the remaining melted butter, cracker crumbs, paprika ,pepper, and rest of cheese.
9.Sprinkle crumb topping over casserole.
10.Bake for 30 to 40 minutes, in 350 degree oven until topping browns slightly and corn is bubbly around the edges.

Every great dinner needs a great desert. This custard is a great desert. You can add 2 cups of fresh or frozen fruit to this. Also dried fruit like radians or dried cranberries would be nice. Or a whisky sauce for the adults.

Custard

> ½ c. butter (1 stick), melted
> 6   Eggs
> 2 tablespoons honey
> 1   Tbs. vanilla
> ¼ tsp. salt
> 1/2 cup flour
> {optional} 2 c. fruit, frozen or fresh; enough to make an even layer in an 8x8 pan. Examples: blueberries, mango, cherries, peaches, raspberries, diced apple, blackberries, raisins, strawberries
> {Another option} 1 tsp cinnamon, 1 tsp nutmeg,1 tsp cardamon, 1st all spice

Directions

1. Place butter in an 8x8 pan. Preheat oven while to 350°F.

2. In a bowl, whisk together honey, milk, eggs, vanilla, salt, flour and melted butter.(If adding spice do that here}

3. {if using fruit}Dump your choice of fruit evenly in the pan. Pour the batter on top.

4. Bake 350°F for 35-45 minutes until custard is set. Remove and let rest for a few minutes. As it cools, it will firm up. Enjoy warm or chilled.

If desired melt 1 stick butter.1 cup white sugar and 6 ounces of whisky. Reduce till half mixture is gone. About 30 min on medium heat. Cool and the pour on top.

Most people do not relish curry was a big deal in England during 1890s. So this is a fantastic for a steampunk party.

Curry meat pie
2 pie crust(foodie recipe chapter)
Filling
    1 pound lamb roast cut into 2in cubes
    ½ cup plain flour
    ½ tsp salt
    ¼ cup curry powder
    ¼ tsp ground black pepper
    ¼ cup vegetable oil
    3 onions, chopped
    3 cloves garlic, chopped
    2 tablespoons brown sugar
    2 cups beef stock
Directions
1.Combine the flour, salt, curry powder and pepper in a bowl and toss the meat through.
2.in a large sauté pan heat 1 oil over medium heat. Sauté the onions and garlic until soft but not brown
3.Shake the excess flour from the meat and add meat. browning on all sides.
4.add beef stock and brown sugar. Cover, and reduce heat, simmer for 20 min or until the meat is soft. Then to thicken, cook without the lid for 10 min.
10. Put filling in pie crust.
11. Roll out second dough ball and put on top of pie pan. Melt 2 Tbls butter and brush on crust.
12. In a 375 degree oven bake for one hour.
Tips
Substitute ground beef instead of lamb cubes
Can use pre made crust

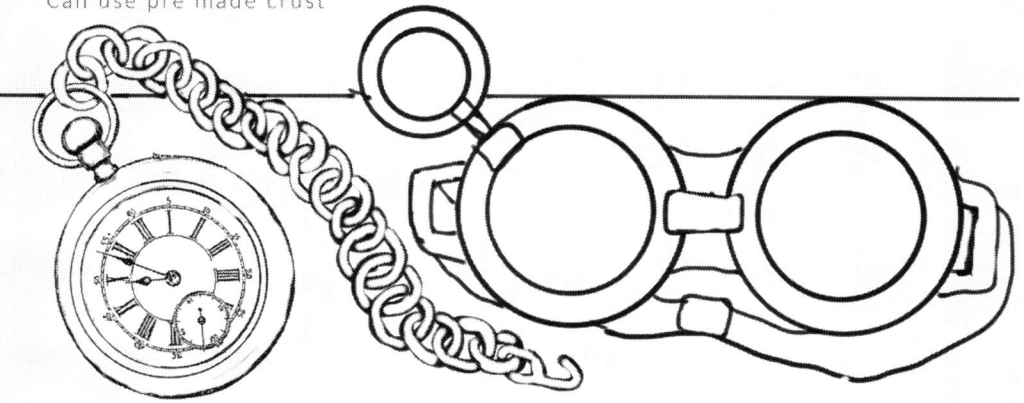

Superhero recipes

Everyone loves a good superhero. Either watching the on tv, movies or reading their adventures. These recipes are more focused on a great meal for a adult superhero party. With a sampling of different cuisines that certain superhero represent. The tips focus more on how to decorate for a adult superhero part or a home watch party.

Every superhero has a hometown, use poster board to create a cityscape backdrop at your food table. Hanging superhero logos around, or the iconic Boom, Thwack signs are also fantastic ways to give homage to the original superhero medium comic books.

If you can spare it, pick up some comic books from a local store to place in the party room.
Purchasing some cut-outs of the superhero, or items with that superheroes theme to put on walls and flat surfaces is also a great idea.

Vinyl tablecloths are not just for tables anymore. They're the superhero of the birthday party supply world, and can also be used as makeshift curtains, doorway hangers, and much more. Get creative with tablecloths and see what you can make the opportunities are endless!

You can have some Superhero Training Set up. Have several stations to test speed, agility, flexibility, strength, and skill. These could include obstacle courses, relay races, throwing skills, target practice or just simple exercises.

You could make the place look like the base of operations for a supergroup. You could cover up tables to make them look like supercomputers, and maybe set up a few prison cells (complete with super-evil inmates) in a corner somewhere. Depending on time constraints and whatnot, you may be able to set up secret passages and what not.

Have plain Capes and mask on hand so people can decorate and wear through the night

I love sushi. This role is good to add to a adult superhero party. This represents all our favorite water based hero's.

Atlantis sushi role
INGREDIENTS
Nori
1/2 pound carrots julienned fine
1 avocado julienned fine
1 package Japanese rice
2 tablespoon Rice wine vinegar

For dipping sauce
1/2 cup sarcha
1/2 fish sauce
1 table spoon lime juice
3 table mustard

Directions

1. make rice as directed on package
2. When rice is finished add rice wine vinegar and stir, set aside
3. Lay out a piece of plastic wrap. Put nori on wrap
4. Place a layer of rice on noir leaving one inch on one side.
5. Place carrots and avocado Down length ways.
6. Roll staring on side without gap. Use water to seal

Add all ingredients for dipping sauce

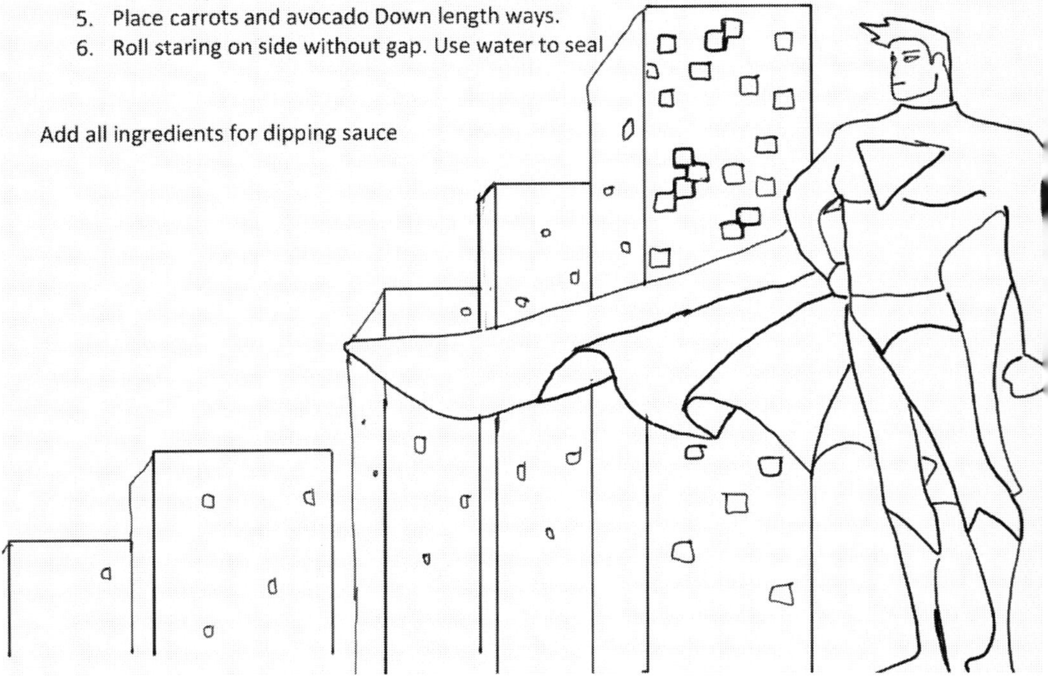

The Norse gods bring a lot to the superhero world. This stew celebrates the brave warriors of the Norse world. This is a great center piece for a great winter meal. Also it rounds out this superhero meal very easily.

Asgardians heroes stew

Ingredients

- 2 cups beef broth
- 2 lbs beef with bone for broth
- 1 lb carrot
- 1 small rutabaga
- 3 cups potatoes (chopped)
- 1 onion finely chopped
- salt
- pepper
- 2 2/3 cup of wild mushrooms, such as chanterelles
- Blueberries or lingonberries

Beef broth

INGREDIENTS

- 1/4 cup vegetable oil
- 4 pounds meaty beef bones
- 1 large onion, sliced
- 4 quarts water

PREPARATION

1. Heat oil in large pot over high heat. Sprinkle bones with salt and pepper. Add bones and onion to pot. Sauté until bones and onion are deep brown, turning often, about 20 minutes. Add 4 quarts water and bring to boil. Reduce heat to medium-low and simmer uncovered until stock is reduced to 3 to 4 cups, about 3 1/2 hours. Strain, discarding bones and onion. DO AHEAD: Can be made 3 days ahead. Refrigerate uncovered until cold, then cover and keep chilled. Spoon off and discard all fat before using.

This drink is strong with a great flavor. This is a drink to prove ones power and bravery. To make it more adult and 2 shots of rum or vodka. This is great to use as a game for kids or just a great non alcoholic punch.

Tribe royal drink of courage
Ingredients

- 3 large ginger roots
- 6limes
- 2–3 cups of water
- 1 tbsp peppercorns
- 1 tbsp raw sugar

Instructions
Leaving the skin on, chop the ginger into small pieces. Chop lime with rind into small chunks.

In a blender, put more ginger than lime and add enough water to be able to blend it. Taste the mixture as you go and add more lime or ginger as needed.

Strain the mixture through a sieve into a bowl and squeeze remaining juice from the pulp.

In the blender add peppercorns and sugar, then return the strained liquid to the blender and blend until smooth.

Once more strain the mixture through a sieve into a saucepan.

Heat the saucepan and bring the liquid to the boil. As soon as the liquid has reached boiling point take it off the heat and allow to cool.

Pour liquid over ice and add a little cold water and drink!

Cookies from space. This are tribute to our favorite super man. This cookies have a crunch from the the homemade candy that resembles a certain green space rock.

Space rocks cookies

Ingredients

Rock candy

- 2 Cups sugar
- 1 Teaspoon baking soda
- 1/4 Cup plus 1 teaspoon citric acid
- 1/2 Cup light corn syrup
- 1/4 Cup water
- 1 Teaspoon vanilla extract
- 1-2 drops food green coloring
- Pinch of cornstarch, for dusting

Cookie

- 1 cup sugar
- 1 cup butter or margarine, softened
- 1 teaspoon vanilla
- 1 egg
- 1 cups Gold Medal™ all-purpose flour
- 1/2 teaspoon baking soda

Directions

Candy

Lightly dust the back side of a baking sheet with cornstarch.

In a medium saucepan, combine the sugar, corn syrup, and water. Cook the mixture until it reaches 300 degrees when measured with a candy thermometer. Remove from heat, and add the baking soda, ¼ cup of the citric acid, extract, and food coloring, and stir to combine.

Spread the mixture out onto the baking sheet (carefully so that it does not run over the edges), sprinkle with the teaspoon of citric acid, and allow to cool completely, about 30 minutes. Break the candy into pieces and add to a Ziploc bag. Using a rolling pin, crush the candy into tiny little pieces put aside

Cookie
Heat oven to 375°F. Line cookie sheet with Reynolds Parchment Paper; set aside.

Paradise island garden pie

This made training style recipe celebrate all the great superhero from the great islands and jungles of the world. This is great to have your little power prince or princes to eat their veggies and maybe get a power up out of it.

INGREDIENTS

for the spinach and feta filling

16 oz chopped spinach

2 bunches flat leaf parsley

1 yellow onion, chopped

2 garlic cloves, minced

2 eggs

10 oz feta cheese crumbled

Pie crust (in foodie recipes)

INSTRUCTIONs

1.In a mixing bowl put all filling ingredients in and mix well with hands.
2.either use pre made crust or make crust from recipe.
3.put crust in pan first, then place filling on top.
4.bake at 325 for an hour. Crust should be light brown.

Tip

You can do this in either muffin pans or minty muffin pan. You may need extra dough for this because of different surface area.

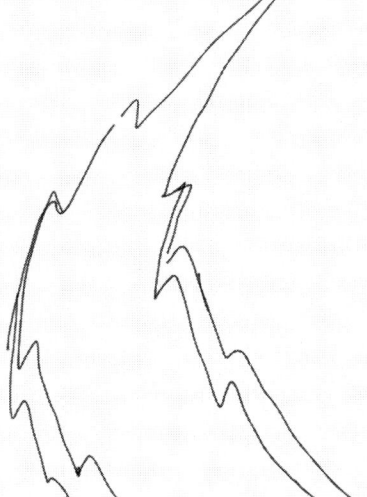

SNACK RECIPES

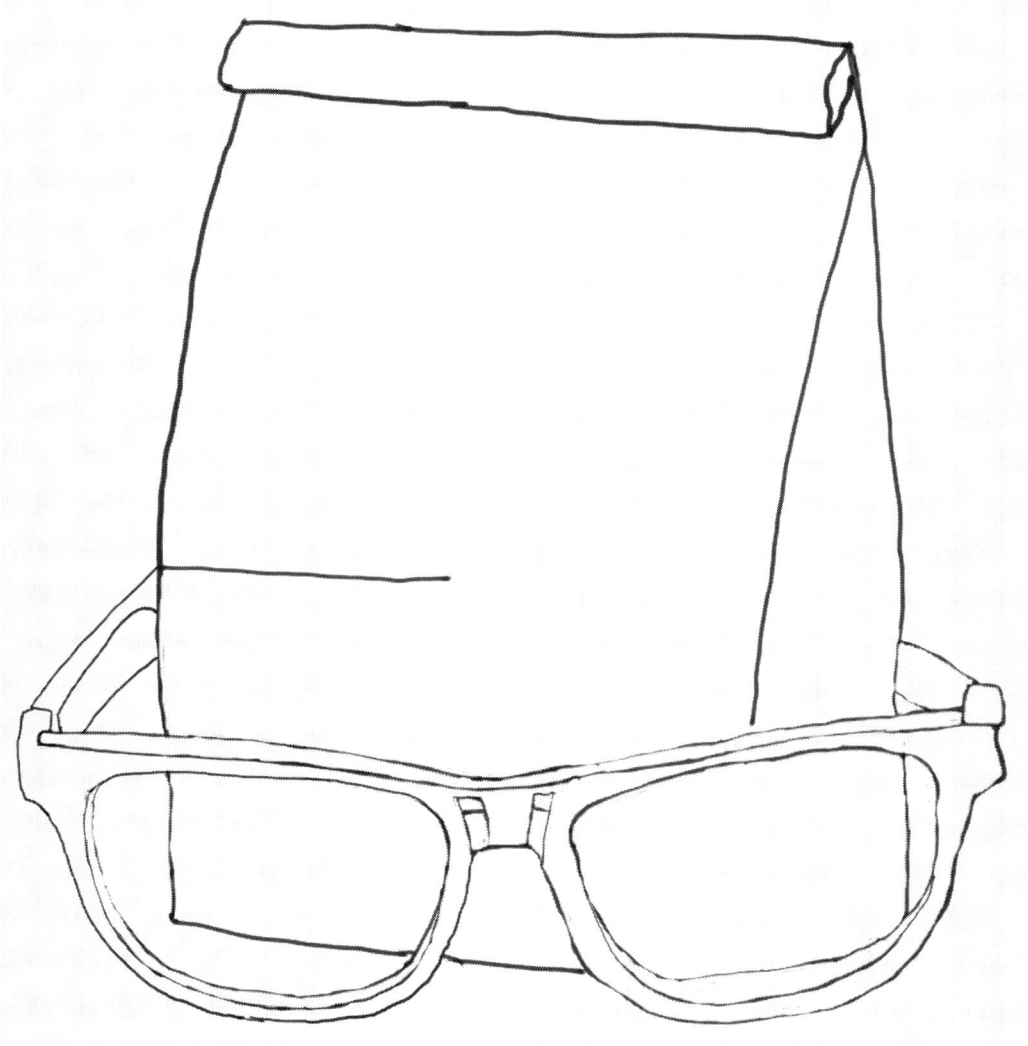

Snacks

This chapter is a little different. These are some great snack or party treats you can make at home with your kid or other little nerds in your life. Instead of a full meal thses are great for a great tv watching session or just some nerds lounging at home. The ideas are not as much party tips but serving ideas and activities to do with theses great nerd snacks.

A lot of these recipes are great to do with kids. There are several ingredients that can be made from scratch. This is where kids can. Get in the kitchen and help with the recipes.

You can easily do a 80s or 90s party with these. Watch some cartoons from the 80s or 90s. Serve food in plastic lunch boxes and drink out of plastic thermos. Use red fruit punch to drink.

Scooby snack
This recipe is actually safe for you and your dog. You can use regular oil but that is not good for your animal. You can serve this in a doggie bowl as a snack or take a old cereal box. Cover in with paper and put your favorite scooby design on it.

biscuits:
1cup pumpkin
½ cup peanut butter
2   Eggs
¼ cup coconut oil*
2½ cups whole wheat flour
1   teaspoon baking soda

Glaze:
tablespoons bacon grease, melted
¼ cup smooth peanut butte

INSTRUCTIONS

1. Preheat oven to 350 degrees.
2. Combine pumpkin, peanut butter, eggs, and oil in a bowl. Add in baking soda and whole wheat flour. Stir until a stiff dough forms. Knead dough or mix just until flour is incorporated.
3. Roll out dough with a rolling pin and use a cookie cutter to cut out round shapes, or just bake into little circles like cookies. Bake for 15 minutes.
4. Whisk the bacon grease and peanut butter until very smooth. Drizzle over the treats and cool till glaze hardens (it does best in the fridge or freezer).

Turkish delight

This is a British candy recipe that is featured in several British fantasy novels. A candy thermometer would be great to have. Also relies on the weather because this will effect your candy making. The orange juice can be switched out for rose water which is traditional. You can also use lemon or lime juice.

- 1 1/2 cups water
- 3 cups granulated sugar
- 3 tablespoons light corn syrup
- 1/2 cup orange juice
- 3 tablespoons orange zest
- 3 (.25 ounce) envelopes unflavored gelatin
- 3/4 cup cornstarch
- 1/2 cup cold water
- 1 tablespoon vanilla extract
- 3/4 cup chopped pistachio nuts
- confectioners' sugar for dustinG

Directions

1. Bring 1 1/2 cups water, sugar, and corn syrup to a boil over medium-high heat in a large saucepan. Cook, stirring frequently, until the temperature reaches 240 degrees F (115 degrees C) on a candy thermometer. Set aside and keep hot.
2. Stir together orange juice and orange zest, sprinkle with gelatin, and set aside. In a small bowl, dissolve cornstarch in 1/2 cup cold water, then stir into hot syrup. Place over medium-low heat, and simmer, stirring gently, until very thick.
3. Remove syrup from heat, stir in orange juice mixture, vanilla, and pistachios. Sprinkle a 8x8-inch pan generously with confectioners' sugar. Pour the Turkish delight into the pan, and let cool in a cool, dry place (not the refrigerator) until set, 3 to 4 hours.
4. When cool, sprinkle the top with another thick layer of powdered sugar. Cut into 1-inch squares, and dredge each well with confectioners' sugar. Store at room temperature in an airtight container.

Elf bread

If your on a long adventure to the land of halflings and trolls. Watching a great fantasy movie for just want to put on some pointy ears and hang with you elf buddies. This elf bread is a great snack. Either by itself or with hunny or butter. A easy to make snack.

1 cup butter
½ cup brown sugar or ¼ cup honey
2 cups unbleached flour

Instructions

1. Preheat oven to 325 degrees.
2. Cream together the butter and sugar or honey. Add the flour and mix until thoroughly incorporated. Put out on suitable surface and knead until quite smooth, about 5 minutes, adding a bit of flour if necessary to keep dough from sticking.
3. Roll out to about ¼ inch thickness and cut into 3" to 4" squares, scoring with a knife halfway through each square with a butter knife. Place on buttered cookie sheet and bake for about 20 to 25 minutes, or until lightly golden brown.

Tip: a great way to serve this is to either find some real big leaves. Lightly rinse and dry the outside. Wrap each peace of bread. Tie it off with a little rope. Also you can take Green Crate paper. Trace a large leaf. Use a strip of ribbion and tie it up. That way you ready for a great adventure

Unicorn dropping cookies

Every one loves unicorns. This is a fun cookie recipe. You can actually use a remade sugar cookie dough but you need to use more food coloring. And why do they look like droppings. Why not? You can use this as just a snack for any fun occasion. If your a Brony, this is a great cookie to watch with your show. But come on unicorn dropping cookies. Nothing better.

- 1 cup Sugar
- 1/2 cup Butter - Softened
- 1/2 cup Shortening
- 3 1/2 tablespoons Cream Cheese - Softened
- 1/2 teaspoon Salt
- 1 whole Egg
- 1/2 teaspoon Almond Extract
- 2 cups All Purpose Flour
- Food Coloring (As many different colors as you want the cookies to be!) the brighter the better

Directions

1. Combine butter, shortening and cream cheese in a large bowl, beat together until smooth. Add sugar and salt. Beat until combined. Beat in egg and almond extract until combined and gradually add the flour beating until combined.
2. Form dough into a ball with your hands and then into a log shape, divide the log shape into six portions (or how ever many colors you want).
3. Place each portion of dough into individual wraps of plastic and tint the dough different colors
4. Get a large piece of plastic wrap (to protect your hands and table from the dye), place a ball of cookie dough in the middle.
5. Poke a well in the center with your thumb.
6. Add the food coloring to the well and then fold the dough over the coloring.
7. Wrap it in the plastic wrap, and begin kneading the food coloring into your dough.
8. This may take a while and you may find that you need more food coloring (Hint: Colored Cookie Dough bakes lighter than what you see when you first tint the dough, once you've gotten the right color tint, add more).
9. Chill tinted dough in the refrigerator 1 hour or freezer 15-20 minutes.
10. Divide each tinted chilled dough ball into 8 equal pieces.
11. Take one piece of each colored dough (leaving the rest in the fridge while you work) and roll out like a rope or snake on your counter-top. If you use a piece of waxed paper on the counter, you shouldn't have to add any flour.
12. Roll the rope shape to about 6 inches long. Continue rolling all the colors and stacking them into a pile. Gently press the ropes together and roll the large multicolored "rope" on the counter to round and smooth it and if desired to lengthen it to 10 to 12".

Tmnt pizza snacks

The turtles love their pizza. The toppings may be a little strange but try them first. You may be surprised. The pepperoni,sweet pickle and cheese is great. The sausage and tomato strawberry jam is a great combo of sweet and spicy. In this recipe you can substitute a lot. The pizza dough , jam, pickle and sausage can all be premade. I think the time is worth it.

*Pepperoni ,Sweet pickles and onions, Mozzarella cheese
1 pizza dough (foodie chapter)
ounces thin sliced pepperoni
12 ounces shredded mozzarella
1 cup pizza sauce (foodie chapter)
Pickle and onions (foodie chapter)
Directions
1.Role out pizza dough to a large square.
2.Use knife to cutout 2inch squares. Add sause on one side leavening a small edge to seal when fold
3.Add cheese to sauce side,, then add pepperoni and add pickles and onions. Fold the plan side to the filling side.
4.Put on dry cooking sheet, about a half inch apart.
Cook at 350 for 30 min.

*strawberry tomato jelly, sausage
1 pizza dough
1 pound cooked sausage.
10 ounce strawberry tomato jam.
10 oUnce blue cheese
Direction
1.Role out pizza dough to a large square.
2.Use knife to cutout 2inch squares. Add jelly on one side leavening a small edge to seal when folded.
3. Add cooked sausage then blue chees. Fold and put on cookie sheet. Cook for 30 mins at 350.

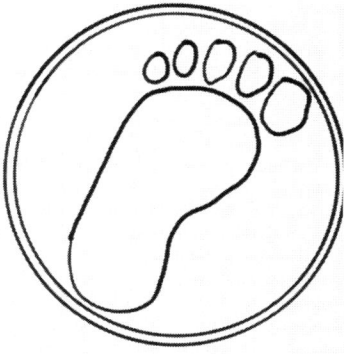

Printed in Great Britain
by Amazon